# GREAT WESTERN RAILWAY STATIONS

## Paddington to Penzance
## via Bristol

Allen Jackson

AMBERLEY

Art deco tiling and Portland stone facings at Bristol Temple Meads.

First published 2017

Amberley Publishing
The Hill, Stroud,
Gloucestershire, GL5 4EP

www.amberley-books.com

ISBN: 978 1 4456 7011 9 (print)
ISBN: 978 1 4456 7012 6 (ebook)

British Library Cataloguing in Publication Data.
A catalogue record for this book is available from the British Library.

Typeset in 10pt on 13pt Celeste.
Origination by Amberley Publishing.
Printed in the UK.

# Introduction

Let's make it clear from the outset that this book is about the railway company that existed from 1835 to 1947, albeit in a recent context. The re-branding of the Train Operating Company (TOC) First Great Western to Great Western Railway inevitably features from time to time as it is their trains in some of the photographs and where this is the case the TOC will be designated as Great Western in the book as distinct from the original GWR.

It can be no exaggeration to say that the GWR has had more words written about it than any other railway company either in the UK or elsewhere. The company engendered enduring interest and affection from those, most of whom nowadays, who never knew the company whilst it was operating. The company was not the largest and neither did it have the streamlined expresses of the 1930s nor a world speed record.

The publicity department at Paddington is often cited as the reason and that is part of the story. The railway existed as one entity for 112 years and even at nationalisation in 1948 the GWR engines kept their original numbers to save the cost of all those brass number plates to be re-done. The railway also had extraordinary visual appeal across all its buildings, structures, locomotives, rolling stock and semaphore signals. Even more than this, the company was a family that looked after its own and gave its employees a sense of belonging and usually a job for life, which many took up and were grateful for.

An old GWR employee who worked in the stores at Swindon recounted the tale of a particularly strict permanent way inspector who happened to be by the water troughs at Goring-on-Thames when a Castle hauled express thundered past and deluged him with the collateral water spray from a locomotive at speed picking up a few thousand gallons. Word of this event spread by the GWR telegraph system at warp speed and the inspector was inundated with waterproof clothing sent from all parts of the railway.

The legendary James Miller at Oxford, a man with the customer service gene firmly embedded, and more recently Norman Topson MBE at Twyford exemplify the high quality service that the GWR gave its passengers, although Norman Topson was too young to know the old company his father had worked for at Henley-on-Thames.

The GWR structure colours of light stone and dark stone have made a comeback in recent years and the network looks more like the old GWR than it has for many years.

The book is arranged in terms of journeys and diagrams of the routes are included.

# Listed Buildings

Many GWR structures are considered to have Architectural and historic merit and are either Grade I or Grade II listed by Historic England. This means they cannot be changed without permission. A Grade I listing would require the interiors to remain as built and some buildings have qualified, notably at Paddington station.

Windsor and Eton Central station houses this replica of the GWR broad gauge engine *The Queen*.

# Summary of Contents

Some stations' names have been modified, usually shortened, in recent years but the old GWR names have been used.

## Paddington to Bristol Temple Meads

Paddington
Hanwell and Elthorne
Southall
West Drayton and Yiewsley
Iver
Langley
Slough and branch to Windsor and Eton Central
Burnham Beeches
Taplow
Maidenhead and branch to Bourne End for Marlow
Twyford
Reading
Tilehurst
Pangbourne
Goring & Streatley
Cholsey & Moulsford
Didcot
Swindon
Chippenham
Bath Spa
Bristol Temple Meads

## Bristol to Plymouth

Yatton
Weston-super-Mare
Bridgwater
Taunton
Exeter St David's
Exeter St Thomas
Starcross
Dawlish Warren
Dawlish
Teignmouth
Newton Abbot and branch to Torre
Torquay
Paignton
Totnes

## Plymouth to Penzance

Royal Albert Bridge
Saltash
Liskeard
Bodmin
Lostwithiel
Par and branch to St Blazey
St Austell
Truro and branch to Falmouth Docks
Redruth
Camborne
St Erth
Penzance

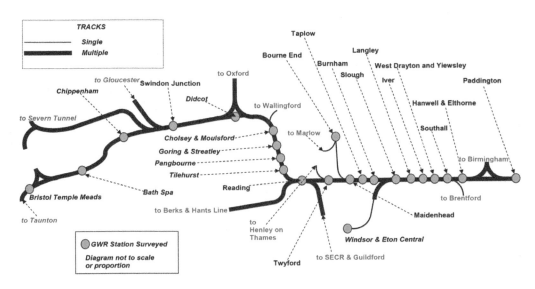

As there is a preponderance of suburban stations nearer London the scale and proportion of Figure 1 has been adjusted to suit but the mileages appended after every journey stop give the true separation.

## Paddington

| Date Built | Railway/Design | Platforms | Passengers 2014–15 | Listed |
|------------|----------------|-----------|--------------------|--------|
| 1854 | GWR/Isambard Kingdom Brunel | 14 | 35.7 million | Grade 1 (part) |

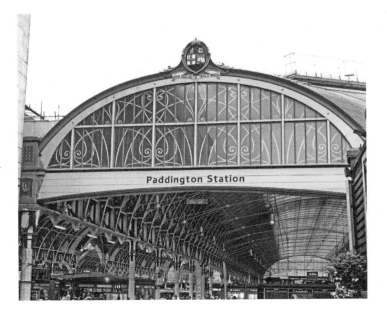

Figure 2 illustrates the view obtained by many passengers over the years at the Praed Street entrance. The coat of arms of London and Bristol surmounts the elegant train shed portico and the theme is continued with 'GW' cast into the ironwork for the roof support on the left. The entrance leads on to 'The Lawn', the circulating area behind the buffer stops. The modernist hotel of the 1930s on the left has the GWR monogram picked out in red. (July 2016).

Figure 3 looks across from The Lawn to platform 1 on the left with the famous clock that in GWR publicity photographs would indicate just before 10:30 and the departure of the Cornish Riviera Limited. The train of that name now leaves from platform 8 and calls at Reading as its first stop whereas a coach would have been slipped for Reading in GWR days. The Stationmaster's balcony on the left is part of the complex of GWR headquarters structures that included the GWR Boardroom and HM Queen Victoria's waiting room for use when royalty were on their way to Windsor. (July 2016).

Figure 4 is the Stationmaster's balcony on platform 1 and Historic England describe it thus: 'elaborate triple oriel with arched openings and Moorish style ironwork'. Many a top-hatted stationmaster must have scrutinised top trains and their departure times from that eyrie-like post. (July 2016).

The inscription reads: 'In honour of those who served in the World Wars 1914–1918, 1939–1945. 25,479 men of the Great Western Railway joined His Majesty's forces, 2,254 gave their lives.'

In the Second World War railways were a reserved occupation that precluded the call up and some railway employees were questioned by members of the public as to their lack of military uniform. This criticism led to all the big four railway companies issuing lapel badges that were inscribed with the company initials and the legend 'For Railway Service'. There were many instances of heroic actions by railway employees in both World Wars that merited civilian decorations and medals.

Beyond the memorial is Great Western's First Class waiting room that emulates airlines with complimentary drinks and food, WiFi and train information. Great Western have used the GWR's art deco 'shirt button' monogram on the windows of the waiting room.

Platform 1 has a bronze sculpture of the character from the Paddington Bear books and no doubt this is a counter to Platform 9¾ at Kings Cross station from the Harry Potter volumes where the platform even has a shop. (July 2016).

Figure 6. A view across from the footbridge that spans platforms 1 to 8 and Class 43 HSTs abound except for the yellow-nosed Class 180 Adelante Diesel Multiple Unit (DMU), which is used on the Cotswold Line services to Worcester and Hereford. (July 2016).

Figure 7. Features a line-up of five Class 43 HSTs and there is one Class 165/6 lurking under the platform awning. The BRISTOL decal on the Class 43 might be a customer relations own goal when it is remembered that some GWR 4-4-0 passenger engines before the First World War had to be renamed as some passengers were confusing the brass nameplates with the train's destination. The GWR office block on Eastbourne Terrace on the platform 1 side of the station in the background is part of the Historic England listing. (July 2016).

Figure 8. Isambard Kingdom Brunel's (IKB) statue looks out from platforms 8 and 9 towards the stationmaster's window on platform 1. The subsidiary arch at right angles to the main train shed extends from platforms 1 to 8 and there is another further arch up to the right. It is a sign of the times that IKB is looking towards McDonald's and Boots. (July 2016).

Figure 9. A less glamorous part of Paddington station is the island containing platforms 13 and 14 which house Thames Valley local trains of about four cars. (July 2016).

Figure 10. The Great Western Royal Hotel at Praed Street Paddington effectively closes off The Lawn end of the station. It is now owned by the Hilton group, which is Conrad as opposed to Paris. The art deco GWR 'shirt button' monogram above the modern entrance awning was used for locomotives and coaches from 1934. The architect was Philip Charles Hardwick. (July 2016).

Figure 11. The legend 'G.W.R. PADDINGTON G.W.R.' can be made out at the top of the early 1930s hotel extension. Most of the other big four railway companies had their logos and other identifying signage removed by BR but the GWR's lives on. (July 2016).

Paddington buffer stops are regarded as the beginning of the GWR system and are therefore measured at 0 miles and 0 chains.

**Hanwell and Elthorne**

| Date Built | Railway/Design | Platforms | Passengers 2014–15 | Listed |
|---|---|---|---|---|
| 1870 circa | GWR/Isambard Kingdom Brunel | 3 Faces (2 in use) | 0.46 million | Grade 2 |

Figure 12. The island platform at Hanwell and Elthorne is surviving well, with the GWR structure colours of light and dark stone making a comeback. Light stone has been described as a creamy buff colour and dark stone a salmon pink. (May 2012).

Figure 13. There is genuine spear fencing at Hanwell and Elthorne which we can see on the left. The station building appears iceberg-like on the platform where only about one third of it is visible and the rest below platform level. The intricate woodwork on the end of the station building, painted white, supported a wooden waiting shelter to supplement the awning. (May 2012).

Figure 14. The rest of the iceberg reveals a contrast between the economical wooden building of the platform level, which has given way to brick when it comes to the stairways and support for the lower levels. Note how the brickwork is embellished with orange and blue bricks as decorative features and this extends to the chimney stack. (May 2012).

Figure 15. Replica signage complete with the pointing finger enhances the GWR feel. The GWR always emphasised what they felt to be the important bits of the message by an increase in font size. Note the decorative orange brickwork and the cast drainpipe let into the masonry. (May 2012).

Figure 16 depicts the island platform 2 again with the unused platform 1 beyond. There are three faux gas lamps from within the canopy. The running-in board has the old GWR name and the company did not seem to use the ampersand or '&' character much, preferring to use the word 'and' in full. (May 2012).

Hanwell and Elthorne station is 7 miles and 28 chains (11.83 km) from Paddington.

**Southall**

| Date Built | Railway/Design | Platforms | Passengers 2014–2015 | Listed |
|---|---|---|---|---|
| Rebuilt 1876 | GWR/Isambard Kingdom Brunel | 5 Faces (4 in use) | 2.31 million | No |

The original road-level station building had three French pavilion-style flat top roofed sections with decorative iron trellis work on the tops and as we can see from Fig. 17, only two have survived and without iron. There is some iron bracketry over the main door to support the small canopy. (July 2016).

Figure 18. The third French pavilion-styled building is more obviously missing in this view where the original covered stairway on the right has also gone. This was done in the late 1970s. (July 2016).

Figure 19. The engine shed or motive power depot is a 1953 replacement for the original 1884 structure and now houses some of West Coast Railway's steam, diesel and coaching stock; the rest are usually at Carnforth. In the yard are a Class 08 shunter, Class 47 500 *County of Essex* and Class 33 'Crompton' as well as coaching stock. (July 2016).

Figure 20. The goods shed at Southall was hanging on in there although long since out of railway use. Within twelve months of the survey date, it'll be out of any use as the whole site is to be cleared.

The plaque on the end wall of the goods shed office is in commemoration of what some of the employees did in the First World War. The fact that two of them won the Military Medal says all that needs to be said. (July 2016).

Figure 21. The former GWR coal stage has survived just because it also houses the water tank to feed the water column on the right. The side facing the camera was where the coal tubs were tipped into tenders and bunkers and you can easily see where the side has been bricked up and later windows inserted. (July 2016).

Figure 22 is a general view from the street level of the lines towards Paddington. The goods shed is at the centre left and is just being passed by the Class 165/6 DMU. (July 2016).

Figure 23 is the other side of the station from the previous one and the building on platform 4 is nearest to us. The Arches Business Centre, formerly a margarine factory, is on the right. (July 2016).

Southall station is 9 miles and 6 chains (14.6 km) from Paddington.

## West Drayton and Yiewsley

| Date Built | Railway/Design | Platforms | Passengers 2014–15 | Listed |
|---|---|---|---|---|
| Rebuilt 1884 | GWR/Isambard Kingdom Brunel | 5 faces (4 in use) | 2.06 million | No |

Figure 24 and the north station building at West Drayton station still has its ironwork in place. (July 2016).

Figure 25 shows the opposite side of the track's entry to the ticket office side in the previous figure and now on platform 1. Note how, when the windows were removed, the bricking up was in the original colour bricks complete with orange decorative bricks as well. (July 2016).

Figure 26 is back on platform 4 side and the removal of the canopy is on the side of what would have been the Staines and Uxbridge (Vine Street) platform 5 branch lines. Note how the ironwork is melded into the decorative brickwork despite a struggle to see this in service. (July 2016).

West Drayton and Yiewsley station is 13 miles and 17 chains (21.26 km) from Paddington.

**Iver**

| Date Built | Railway/Design | Platforms | Passengers 2012–13 | Listed |
|---|---|---|---|---|
| 1924 | GWR | 4 faces (2 in use) | 0.186 million | No |

Figure 27. Into Buckinghamshire now and Iver was a latecomer to the scene; the plain nature of the buildings reflects harder railway times. The nearer high speed platforms are fenced off.

Figure 28. The ticket office at Iver is still doing the same job it was built to do in 1924 and the GWR corrugated iron school of architecture exemplified by pagoda sheds has moved into station buildings.

Iver station is 14 miles and 60 chains (23.74 km) from Paddington.

## Langley

| Date Built | Railway/Design | Platforms | Passengers 2012–13 | Listed |
|---|---|---|---|---|
| 1845 | GWR/Isambard Kingdom Brunel | 4 faces (2 in use) | 0.72 million | No |

Figure 29. Modern East Berkshire and Langley station building looks fairly original apart from the vegetation. The decorative ironwork, chimneys and canopy valence look original. The building no longer has any public railway function. (July 2016).

Figure 30. Langley is a story of two stations in the sense that the high speed platforms are fenced off and no longer used. The HST Class 43 speeds to Slough and the west. The Langley oil depot is to the right and was last used by EWS. (July 2016).

Langley station is 16 miles and 18 chains (26.11 km) from Paddington.

## Slough

| Date Built | Railway/Design | Platforms | Passengers 2012–13 | Listed |
|------------|----------------|-----------|--------------------|--------|
| 1884 | GWR/ J. E. Danks | 6 faces | 5.6 million | Yes |

Figure 31. This distinctive Second Empire French style with the mansard roof was only emulated at one other GWR station and in a lesser manner. Queen Victoria used to come here before she got her own station at Windsor. (July 2016).

Figure 32. This effusive and grand style was carried on at the opposite side to the main entrance and there are three buildings at Slough station mentioned by Historic England in the listing. (July 2016).

Figure 33. The island platform layout with canopies has been extended to three platform groups with the Windsor bay nearest to the camera. The far platform has a modernised canopy. Note the DMU exhaust staining on the Windsor bay canopy, which is platform 1. (July 2016).

Figure 34. Platform 3 on the left and platform 4 on the right of the same island sit between the fast and slow lines. The two HSTs on the left are giving the fast lines a workout although the 'BRISTOL 2015' set is stopping here. Platform 4 awaits an arrival from Paddington to go on to Reading. Note how the canopies here are two separate structures and are connected by steel girders. There had been a bay platform here between Platforms 3 and 4. The gap between the canopies indicates where the bay platform track was below. (July 2016).

Figure 35. Class 165 108 is at rest at the Windsor bay platform 1. There is another buffer stop next to the platform, which is a legacy of a run-round loop that is no longer needed. Note the over-arching nature of the platform 2 canopy on the left. (July 2016).

Slough station is 18 miles and 36 chains (29.69 km) from Paddington.

The main line journey is now interrupted by a short trip down the branch to Windsor.

## Windsor and Eton Central

| Date Built | Railway/Design | Platforms | Passengers 2012–13 | Listed |
|---|---|---|---|---|
| 1849 Rebuilt 1897 | GWR | 1 face | 1.885 million | Yes |

Figure 36. The Brunel timber train shed of the 1840s was swept away and replaced by a grand terminus on the occasion of Queen Victoria's Diamond Jubilee in 1897. The station shown is described by Historic England as: 'Large terminus station set back behind road line. Pedimented Dutch gable over concourse entrance which has broad segmental glazed girder roof. The main station block is to the right of 2 and 3 storeys deep red brick set on obtuse angle with steep French hipped roof over slightly projecting western end bays.' (January 2007).

Figure 37. The station continues in red brick as described in the previous figure but what it doesn't mention is that below the triangular pediment on the top floor at the front is a relief in brick with the initials of the company. (January 2007).

Figure 38. No expense was spared on the interiors with this fabulously panelled former ticket office with ceramic tiling. Queen Victoria had her own waiting room in a separate building and it is now a restaurant. (January 2007).

Figure 39. The original four platforms were reduced to this one but the station still serves about one third of the number of passengers as Slough on the main line. The familiar round tower of Windsor Castle is in the background and the station road connection is right opposite the large public entrance to the castle. The fencing is of a later period and the whole station platform structures were built up on a viaduct of over a mile in length comprising 257 arches and a bridge over the River Thames. (January 2007).

Windsor and Eton Central station is 21 miles and 19 chains (34.18 km) from Paddington.
   The main line journey is now resumed at Burnham.

**Burnham Beeches**

| Date Built | Railway/Design | Platforms | Passengers 2014–15 | Listed |
|---|---|---|---|---|
| 1899 | GWR | 2 faces | 1.28 million | No |

Figure 40. Back down to earth from the regal splendour of Windsor and Burnham has a station that is only served by the relief or slow lines. (September 2016).

Figure 41. The station building is an earlier rendition of one of the GWR standard station buildings with the rounded corners picked out in engineer's blue brick. The view is towards Slough and Paddington. Burnham Beeches featured in a book by Hugh Page published by the GWR in 1937 entitled *Rambles in the Chiltern Country*; at the time Burnham was in Buckinghamshire. (September 2016).

Burnham station is 20 miles and 77 chains (33.74 km) from Paddington.

## Taplow

| Date Built | Railway/Design | Platforms | Passengers 2012–13 | Listed |
|------------|----------------|-----------|--------------------|--------|
| 1872 | GWR/J. E. Danks | 4 faces | 0.239 million | No |

Figure 42. Back into Buckinghamshire and the GWR went back into four-platform mode at Taplow; this was the terminus of the line for a while pending the building of Maidenhead Bridge over the River Thames. The present station dates from the line's quadrupling when it was mixed broad and standard gauge. Although there are four platforms, there are now only station buildings on the relief lines. The 1884 built footbridge connects the pairs of lines. (May 2006).

Figure 43. The main station building on platform 4 is an intricate use of decorative brick and stonework and that round the windows has been done twice over. This is yet another example of building to impress others as some of the directors of the GWR lived nearby and Taplow was their local station. It is also scandalously close to Cliveden. (May 2006).

Figure 44. On the other side of the footbridge was the West Signal Cabin, which backed onto the footbridge at right angles to the running lines but closed in 1930. (May 2006).

Figure 45. The detail and work carried out on the main station building was carried through to this waiting shelter on platform 3. The original spear fencing in the foreground has been made into a gate. (May 2006).

Taplow station is 22 miles and 39 chains (36.19 km) from Paddington.

**Maidenhead**

| Date Built | Railway/Design | Platforms | Passengers 2013–14 | Listed |
|---|---|---|---|---|
| 1871 | GWR/William Woodbridge | 5 faces | 4.2 million | No |

Figure 46. Maidenhead seems to have reverted to the London yellow bricks with orange decorative effects of earlier in the journey. The station site at the platform 4 side of the station, by the Marlow branch line, is quite cramped and in the middle of the town. Stationers were very common at railway stations and the fact that WH Smith is here still is a statement as to how busy the station remains. (September 2016).

Figure 47. The platform 1 side of Maidenhead station is rather like West Drayton in brickwork style and decoration but there are no bricked up windows here. (September 2016).

Figure 48. Platform 1 is behind the camera and the view is towards platforms 4 and 5. The Class 165 114 is accelerating towards Reading from platform 3. Note how the former Wycombe line leaves the main line to the right just by the last coach of the Class 165. (September 2016).

Figure 49. Platform 5 is the Marlow branch platform where the 'Marlow Donkey' used to depart from in GWR days. The so called Wycombe line no longer goes there but terminates at Bourne End and trains then reverse to Marlow from there. (September 2016).

Maidenhead station is 24 miles and 19 chains (39 km) from Paddington.
The journey now deviates north up the Wycombe line to Bourne End.

**Bourne End**

| Date Built | Railway/Design | Platforms | Passengers 2013–14 | Listed |
|:---:|:---:|:---:|:---:|:---:|
| 1854 | Wycombe | 2 faces | 0.25 million | No |

Figure 50. Bourne End station looking towards High Wycombe but now there are only buffer stops. The knapped flint goods shed is still earning its keep on the right. (September 2016).

Figure 51. A closer look at Bourne End station building with the attractive knapped flint/ engineer's blue brick stationmaster's residence at the end and the waiting room on the left, which it still is. There is a GWR platform seat inside the waiting room. There is bullhead railed track with GWR two-bolt chairs. (September 2016).

Figure 52. The Marlow branch curves away to the right whilst the line from Maidenhead comes in from the top of the picture and then splits for the two platforms. The sign on the signal says 'Obtain token or staff before proceeding'. The single-track Marlow branch is worked One Train Staff where a physical piece of wood is the driver's authority to proceed and only one is ever issued. The Maidenhead to Bourne End Section, also single-track, is worked No Signaller Key Token where the train driver obtains a token from a machine and this act locks all the signals in the opposite direction. The signaller at Slough supervises all such branch line operations. This way of working ensures that two trains can operate at peak times thus: Bourne End to Marlow – Platform 1 where the camera is; Maidenhead – Bourne End – Platform 2 opposite side to camera. The points are set for a train from Marlow. (September 2016).

Figure 53. From Platform 2, Class 165 121 arrives from Marlow into platform 1, off peak, and will depart from the same platform. The ground frame hut that contains the key token and other controls is the grey hut on the right of the DMU. Signal BE 1 on the platform will indicate M for Main or Maidenhead upon departure and B for branch if headed for Marlow. (September 2016).

Bourne End station is 28 miles and 55 chains (46.17 km) from Paddington and Marlow is a further 2 miles 54 chains (4.3 km).

## Twyford

| Date Built | Railway/Design | Platforms | Passengers 2013–14 | Listed |
|------------|----------------|-----------|--------------------|--------|
| 1892 | GWR | 5 faces | 1.23 million | No |

Figure 54. The view from Hirst Road in Twyford is of a standard 1892-built station building on platform 1 that was built after the broad gauge was narrowed. The footbridge was also part of the same modernisation process. (November 2005).

Figure 55. The view is from platform 4 and across to platform 5 on the left. The massive canopy is to accommodate the swirling crowds of champagne-fuelled revellers who are on their way to Henley Regatta. The Henley-on-Thames branch, platform 5, is on the left and there are remnants of the cattle pens on the extreme left and this accommodation was shared with the run-round loop for locomotives off the Henley branch. (November 2005).

Figure 56. Platform 1 provides the rostrum for this view across to platforms 4 and 5 with the island platforms 2 and 3 in the middle. Observe the wooden station building detail and the footbridge. (November 2005).

Twyford station is 31 miles and 1 chain (46.17 km) from Paddington.

**Reading**

| Date Built | Railway/Design | Platforms | Passengers 2014–15 | Listed |
|---|---|---|---|---|
| 1860 | GWR | 11 faces (pre-rebuild) | 16.34 million | No |

Figure 57. In 1860 the GWR replaced the rudimentary Brunel timber train shed with this ticket office and main station building in Bath stone and brick, complete with clock tower. (March 2007).

Figure 58. In 1898 the GWR also replaced the existing inadequate platforms and their access with these superb platforms and buildings, capable of handling the longest service trains. By about 2005 the need for long platforms was over, in favour of more platforms, and the decision was taken to rebuild the station. (March 2007).

Figure 59. Platform 10 was handling a Class 165 DMU on local eastbound services in the bay. Note the hydraulic buffer stops and the scaled down proportions of the canopy. (March 2007).

Figure 60. The island platform canopies surrounding platforms 5, 6, 7 and 8 were massive and platform 7 has platform faces for both sides of the train even though the train doors only open on one side. The view is across to platform 3 where trains to the Westbury or 'Berks and Hants' line were dispatched and received. (March 2007).

Reading station is 35 miles and 78 chains (57.9 km) from Paddington.

**Tilehurst**

| Date Built | Railway/Design | Platforms | Passengers 2013–14 | Listed |
|---|---|---|---|---|
| 1882 | GWR | 4 faces | 0.52 million | No |

Figure 61. The view along the fast lines towards Reading reveals the small lockup goods shed. The trailing ladder crossovers connect all running lines. (November 2003).

Figure 62. The small station building on platform 1 was only a ticket office and staff accommodation. Note the stone construction, similar to the goods shed, whereas all other buildings on site are brick. (November 2003).

Figure 63. The small waiting room on the up slow platform has no coal fireplace but it is much later than the rest of the station. However, the brickwork style has been built to be in keeping with the standard island platform building. (November 2003).

Tilehurst station is 38 miles and 52 chains (62.2 km) from Paddington.

**Pangbourne**

| Date Built | Railway/Design | Platforms | Passengers 2013–14 | Listed |
|------------|----------------|-----------|--------------------|--------|
| 1880s | GWR | 2 faces | 0.42 million | No |

Figure 64. The built up nature of Pangbourne station is apparent in this view and the station has a subway rather than a footbridge. The relief lines are the only ones served here and the station building is situated on platform 2. Note the replica gas lamps and original spear fencing as well as paling fencing on the platform. (September 2006).

Figure 65. There were originally four platforms here but the station buildings and services appear to have been removed about the same time as the platform 1 canopy. See the subway entrance on the left and the HST hurtling towards Paddington behind. (September 2006).

Figure 66. Pure Great Westernry in the 'Drive Slowly' sign that has age to it. (September 2006).

Pangbourne station is 41 miles and 43 chains (66.85 km) from Paddington.

## Goring and Streatley

| Date Built | Railway/Design | Platforms | Passengers 2013–14 | Listed |
|---|---|---|---|---|
| 1895 | GWR | 4 faces, 2 in use | 0.399 million | No |

Figure 67. Goring and Streatley station from the B4009 bridge reveals the fast lines on the right with out-of-use platforms and relief or slow lines to the left. (April 2005).

Figure 68. Standard 1890s waiting shelter and toilet block on platforms 3 and 2 and footbridge connection but, unusually, without chimney stacks. The view is towards Didcot. (April 2005).

Goring and Streatley station is 44 miles and 60 chains (72.02 km) from Paddington.

## Cholsey and Moulsford

| Date Built | Railway/Design | Platforms | Passengers 2014–15 | Listed |
|:---:|:---:|:---:|:---:|:---:|
| 1892 | GWR | 5 faces, 3 in use | 0.272 million | No |

Figure 69. Cholsey and Moulsford station track is elevated like Pangbourne and, mindful of the nearby River Thames, this was a wise choice. This is the junction for the Wallingford branch, which is now a heritage railway. (April 2005).

Figure 70. The platforms in use are, from left to right: 5 – Wallingford branch, note the run round loop just in shot; 4 – Up relief line to Paddington, the station building is the one we saw in the previous figure; 3- Down relief to Didcot and Swindon - note no canopies again.

The far platforms are disused as 2 and 1 respectively but a waiting shelter survives. (April 2005).

Figure 71. The way to the west and Didcot and Swindon from platform 4. The Class 165 is heading east towards Paddington on the up main. (April 2005).

Cholsey and Moulsford station is 48 miles and 37 chains (77.99 km) from Paddington.

**Didcot**

| Date Re-Built | Railway/Design | Platforms | Passengers 2014–15 | Listed |
|:---:|:---:|:---:|:---:|:---:|
| 1887 | GWR | 5 faces | 3.5 million | No |

Figure 72. BR closed and sold off Didcot engine shed to the Great Western Society so now the Class 66 and pair of Class 37s have to park in Didcot Yard. Note the GWS water towering above the last Class 66. Power station is in operation. (September 2003).

Figure 73. Some years later and the locos stabled have reduced, possibly due to the collapse in coal traffic, and this is mirrored in the power station's inactivity. The yard is still present and the Oxford line forms a triangle with the GWS in the centre as well as Network Rail tracks. The view is towards Swindon. (September 2016).

Didcot station is 53 miles and 10 chains (85.5 km) from Paddington.

## Swindon Junction

| Date Built | Railway/Design | Platforms | Passengers 2013–14 | Listed |
|---|---|---|---|---|
| 1842 | GWR/Isambard Kingdom Brunel | 4 faces (after 2003) | 3.35 million | No |

Figure 74. The only part of the GWR Swindon station remaining is the island platform and that has three faces. Platform 1 sees a departure for Paddington from a Class 43 HST, entitled *The Red Arrows*, from Cheltenham. Platform 2 on the left is the bay for the line to Westbury and Salisbury. Platform 3 is used for services from Bristol and South Wales. (September 2016).

Figure 75. The canopy arrangement on the island platform 3 is recognisably GWR in origin. Note the oil drums used to protect the columns from the depredations of motorised parcels trollies. (November 2006).

Figure 76. The view to the west to Chippenham and the divergent tracks to the right are to Gloucester and Cheltenham. What remains of Swindon Works is also in view. (September 2016).

Swindon station is 77 miles and 23 chains (124.38 km) from Paddington.

## Chippenham

| Date Built | Railway/Design | Platforms | Passengers 2014–15 | Listed |
|---|---|---|---|---|
| 1858 | GWR/J. H. Bertram | 3 faces 2 in use | 1.9 million | Yes |

Figure 77. Chippenham station is an early delight in Bath stone and the main building on the left is listed. The Calne branch platform ran into an enclave onto the left side of the island platform making this, originally, a four-platform station. (November 2006).

Figure 78. The island platform now sees all trains, including this eastbound HST. (November 2006).

Figure 79. In the station yard is Brunel's office building from which the GWR main line was planned, also listed and said to date from 1840. (November 2006).

Chippenham station is 93 miles and 76 chains (151.2 km) from Paddington.

**Bath Spa**

| Date Built | Railway/Design | Platforms | Passengers 2014–2015 | Listed |
|---|---|---|---|---|
| 1841 | GWR/ Isambard Kingdom Brunel | 2 faces | 6.36 million | Yes |

Figure 80. Brunel designed a station completely in keeping with Bath's Georgian architecture and the local stone. (August 2016).

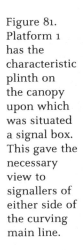

Figure 81. Platform 1 has the characteristic plinth on the canopy upon which was situated a signal box. This gave the necessary view to signallers of either side of the curving main line.

Figure 82. The view from platform 1 amply demonstrates the elevated nature of the line above the city. Passengers are sitting on at least two GWR seats with the 1894 monogram on the castings.

Bath Spa station is 106 miles and 71 chains (172.02 km) from Paddington.

**Bristol Temple Meads**

| Date Built | Railway/Design | Platforms | Passengers 2014–2015 | Listed |
|------------|----------------|-----------|----------------------|--------|
| 1840 | GWR/ Isambard Kingdom Brunel | 13 faces | 11.5 million | Yes Grade 1 |

Figure 83. Bristol Temple Meads station is laid out from the Bath Road bridge. The short dock sidings on the left are for parcels and perishables traffic and are disused. The iconic castellated tower that appears in the next figure is to the left of the train shed and behind that is Brunel's original terminus, which is now a car park. The view is towards Paddington. (August 2016).

Figure 84. The extraordinary decorative stonework is just about matched by the intricacy of the canopy ironwork. (August 2016).

Figure 85. A 1930s update saw the use of smooth tiling and a statement as to where you were – BRISTOL. This kind of decoration was also used at Cardiff General. The Class 150 DMU looks suitably overawed. (August 2016).

Figure 86. The replica lettering style on this figure is from an earlier, pre-First World War era although platforms 13 and 15 (there is no 14) are later. (August 2016).

Figure 87. The pomp and circumstance wasn't just for the façade as this view between the train shed and Brunel's terminus, on the right, shows. The columns are dated 1876. (August 2016).

Figure 88. Brunel's original terminus station 'Passenger Shed' with early signal box on the left. (August 2016).

Bristol Temple Meads station is 118 miles and 31 chains (190.53 km) from Paddington. The journey continues into the West Country and on to Plymouth, Fig. 89.

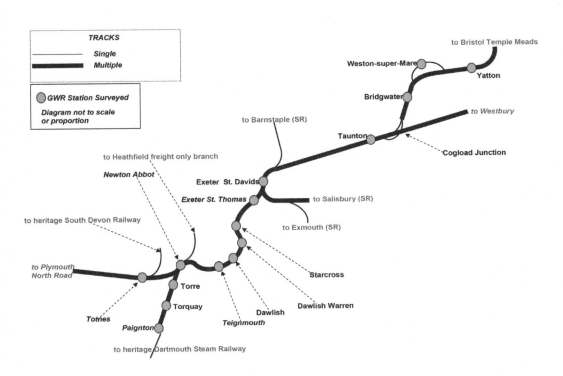

## Yatton

| Date Built | Railway/Design | Platforms | Passengers 2013–2014 | Listed |
|---|---|---|---|---|
| 1841 | Bristol and Exeter Railway/IKB | 2 faces | 0.417 million | Yes |

Figure 90. The footbridge is also listed at Yatton and is thought to date from 1870, so an early example. The feather on the colour light signal is for the down goods loop. (June 2016).

Figure 91. The up station building looking towards Plymouth shows a fine stone building with the former Clevedon branch bay and canopy beyond. The GWR favoured the curved type on narrow platforms. Note the postbox let into the station building wall. (June 2016).

Figure 92. The down station building looking towards Plymouth also harboured the Cheddar Valley branch line bay and the goods yard. Note the 1934 monogrammed GWR platform seats. Light and dark stone GWR colours are in evidence. (June 2016).

Yatton station is 130 miles and 28 chains (209.78 km) from Paddington.

**Weston-super-Mare**

| Date Built | Railway/Design | Platforms | Passengers 2014–2015 | Listed |
|---|---|---|---|---|
| 1884 | B&E  later GWR | 3 faces | 1.1 million | No |

Figure 93. Solid stone construction built to last. The bay platform is not on the timetables but clearly usable. There is a listed B&E signal box in the yard on the right behind the camera. The view is west towards Bridgwater. (August 2016).

Figure 94. Although the station is not a tall building, it is an imposing one with plenty of space for holidaymakers milling about. Weston-super-Mare was the favourite destination for the Swindon 'trip'. (August 2016).

Figure 95. The opposite side entrance is more discrete but, with the parcels and luggage lift towers, still has a presence. (August 2016).

Weston-super-Mare station is 137 miles and 33 chains (221.14 km) from Paddington.

**Bridgwater**

| Date Built | Railway/Design | Platforms | Passengers 2014–2015 | Listed |
|---|---|---|---|---|
| 1841 | Bristol and Exeter Railway/IKB | 2 faces | 0.309 million | Yes |

Figure 96. Bridgwater station has distinctive glazed draught panels at both ends of the canopies. The siding leaving the main line on the up side towards Paddington is the connection to the former docks branch. (August 2016).

Figure 97. A HST set slows down for a station stop at platform 2 on its way to Paddington from Plymouth. There are GWR platform seats and customers at 7.04 a.m. and no litter. (August 2016).

Figure 98. Freight on the Great Western is now rare and the former docks branch at Bridgwater has been adapted to accommodate the nuclear de-commissioning traffic from Hinckley Point power station. Two DRS Class 37 locomotives and two nuclear flasks on wagons are in attendance. (August 2016).

Bridgwater station is 151 miles and 47 chains (221.14 km) from Paddington.

## Taunton

| Date Built | Railway/Design | Platforms | Passengers 2014–2015 | Listed |
|---|---|---|---|---|
| 1864/1932 | B&E/GWR | 6 faces | 1.315 million | Part Grade 2 |

Figure 99. This refreshment room on platform 5 has an art deco look to it and doubtless dates from the line's quadrupling in 1932. (July 2016).

Figure 100. The view across platform 2 has to take in platforms 3 and 4, which had lain derelict for many years under BR. (July 2016).

Figure 101. A familiar landmark at Taunton station is the water tower, which survives as it is now a home. For many years it advertised Van Heusen shirts, which had a factory in the town, and traces of the 'V' can be seen. (July 2016).

Taunton station is 163 miles and 12 chains (262.56 km) from Paddington.

**Exeter St Davids**

| Date Built | Railway/Design | Platforms | Passengers 2014–2015 | Listed |
|---|---|---|---|---|
| 1864 Rebuild | B&E/GWR | 6 faces | 3.44 million | No |

Figure 102. One of the quintessential GWR station buildings complete with the shirt-button monogram just below the triangular pediment. The GWR stamped its authority on the city of Exeter, where it was in competition with the London & South Western Railway. (July 2016).

Figure 103. The view is from Red Cow level crossing. Just beyond the Class 150 the line swings away to the left and the 1 in 37 incline up to Exeter Central station. The HST has arrived from Paddington and is headed for Paignton. (July 2016).

Figure 104. As well as the parcels and luggage lift, whose towers are so prominent in the last picture, there is this behemoth of a footbridge. See how there are two staircases up to the bridge from the island platform. (July 2016).

Figure 105. The broad gauge transhipment shed is the only listed railway building hereabouts and clearly the right-hand opening was for the wider gauge. A Southwestern Trains Class 159 is parked. (July 2016).

Figure 106. The GWR makes another statement about the importance of Exeter St Davids station with bespoke ceramic tiles to make up this charming sign. (July 2016).

Exeter St Davids station is 193 miles and 72 chains (312.05 km) from Paddington via Box.

**Exeter St Thomas**

| Date Built | Railway/Design | Platforms | Passengers 2014–2015 | Listed |
|---|---|---|---|---|
| 1861 Rebuild | South Devon Railway | 2 faces | 0.214 million | Yes |

Figure 107. This later station building post-dates the atmospheric railway terminal and is Grade II listed. (July 2016).

Figure 108. There was a timber west-country overall roof here until the 1960s and the station is elevated on a sixty-six-arch viaduct. The train service is carried out by Class 150 and Class 142 DMUs. (July 2016).

Exeter St Thomas station is 194 miles and 66 chains (313.54 km) from Paddington via Box.

**Starcross**

| Date Built | Railway/Design | Platforms | Passengers 2014–2015 | Listed |
|---|---|---|---|---|
| 1845 Pump Hse | South Devon Railway | 2 faces | 101,104 | Yes Grade I |

Figure 109. This Cross Country Trains Voyager DMU powers round the curve past Brunel's atmospheric pumping house and through Starcross station on its way from Plymouth to Edinburgh. (July 2016).

Starcross station is 202 miles and 36 chains (325.81 km) from Paddington via Box.

**Dawlish Warren**

| Date Built | Railway/Design | Platforms | Passengers 2014–2015 | Listed |
|---|---|---|---|---|
| 1905 | GWR | 2 faces | 0.157 million | No |

Figure 110. A Class 43 HST speeds towards Exeter on the up fast line, past the up loop. The structure that resembles a GWR type 7 signal box is a replica built since the original was demolished. The camping coaches, whose last season this was, are just to the right of the nose of the HST. (July 2016).

Figure 111. In the up loop at Dawlish Warren is this Colas Class 70 and track maintenance train that is now leaving the loop after the HST has sped past. (July 2016).

Dawlish Warren station is 204 miles and 37 chains (329.05 km) from Paddington via Box.

**Dawlish**

| Date Built | Railway/Design | Platforms | Passengers 2014–2015 | Listed |
|---|---|---|---|---|
| 1875 | South Devon Railway/ GWR | 2 faces | 0.557 million | Yes |

Figure 112. The station at Dawlish is as close to the beach and the sea as it's possible to get and there are the remains of another atmospheric pumping station here in the car park. (July 2016).

Figure 113. Class 150 accelerates away from a station stop at Dawlish towards the first of five tunnels, Kennaway at 209 yards (191 m), and the next stop at Teignmouth. (July 2016).

Dawlish station is 206 miles and 7 chains (331.67 km) from Paddington via Box.

## Teignmouth

| Date Built | Railway/Design | Platforms | Passengers 2014–2015 | Listed |
|------------|----------------|-----------|----------------------|--------|
| 1895 | South Devon Railway/ GWR | 2 faces | 0.604 million | No |

Figure 114. The three French pavilion-style roofs are reminiscent of Southall before it was modified except that here the building is in stone. (July 2016).

Figure 115. The single-car MU Class 153, 153382, is headed for Newton Abbot from platform 1. Note the BR Western Region seats and older wooden type on the far platform. The wide platforms and expansive canopies were needed for the masses of holidaymakers. Platform 1 can handle a fifteen coach train. (July 2016).

Teignmouth station is 208 miles and 70 chains (336.15 km) from Paddington via Box.

**Newton Abbot**

| Date Built | Railway/Design | Platforms | Passengers 2014–2015 | Listed |
|---|---|---|---|---|
| 1927 | South Devon Railway/GWR | 3 faces | 1.141 million | No |

Figure 116. South Devon House is an attractive building and a product of the 1927 rebuild. (July 2016).

Figure 117. Modifications to the layout at Newton Abbot did away with platform 4, the loco depot, and the South Devon Railway Works. The Class 150 is on its way to Exmouth from Paignton. The right-hand track leads to the former Aller Junction and the Paignton/Kinswear branch. (July 2016).

Figure 118. This Cross Country Voyager DMU is zooming along from Newcastle to Plymouth and is on schedule as it passes through Newton Abbot station. Note that the platform buildings are of mostly timber construction. (July 2016).

Figure 119. Looking to the east end of the station, on the left are the remains of platform 4 and further up the line the Heathfield branch diverges. Tucker's Maltings are on the left. (July 2016).

Newton Abbot station is 214 miles and 5 chains (344.5 km) from Paddington via Box. The journey now takes in the branch line to Paignton.

**Torre**

| Date Built | Railway/Design | Platforms | Passengers 2014–2015 | Listed |
|---|---|---|---|---|
| 1848/1882 | South Devon Railway/GWR | 2 faces | 274,436 | Yes |

Figure 120. The Brunellian timber station building at Torre is a rare survivor and has been added to over the years and is listed and possibly also listing. (July 2016).

Figure 121. Torre footbridge is also listed but the station building has been boarded up mostly as it is in other use. There is plenty of GWR seating here. Observe the wooden offices for the goods yard beyond the station building. (July 2016).

Figure 122. Torre signal box was closed in the 1980s. Note the rectangular steel frame by the door for six fire buckets. (September 2014).

Torre station is 219 miles and 12 chains (352.69 km) from Paddington via Box.

**Torquay**

| Date Built | Railway/Design | Platforms | Passengers 2014–2015 | Listed |
|---|---|---|---|---|
| 1878 Rebuilt | South Devon Railway/GWR | 2 faces | 0.458 million | Yes |

Figure 123. Another closed signal box survivor on platform 1 at Torquay. The now-removed centre track was called 'Middle Siding'. (July 2016).

Figure 124. The French pavilion roofs complete with ironmongery are more embellished than at Teignmouth, and grander. (September 2014).

Figure 125. Torquay station is underwhelmed by the arrival of a Class 143 Pacer, 143617, on a service from Paignton. Note how the road over bridge at the end of the platforms is painted in the same livery as the station. (July 2016).

Figure 126. Wide platforms and commodious canopies provide protection for the thronging masses of summer visitors and the delightful sub-tropical planting a diversion whilst queuing to get off the station or waiting for the train home. The station building is repeated on platform 2, which is unusual. (July 2016).

Torquay station is 219 miles and 79 chains (354.04 km) from Paddington via Box.

## Paignton

| Date Built | Railway/Design | Platforms | Passengers 2014–2015 | Listed |
|------------|----------------|-----------|----------------------|--------|
| 1924 Rebuilt | South Devon Railway/GWR | 2 faces | 0.632 million | No |

Figure 127. Paignton station sees the start of single track to Dartmouth and, on the far left, the Dartmouth Steam Railway heritage line. The goods shed on the right has been converted into the ticket office. (July 2016).

Figure 128. Class 143 Pacer 143612 waits to set off for Exmouth and as this is effectively a terminus there is a crossover here to allow trains to regain the correct platform before setting off back towards Torquay. (July 2016).

Figure 129. Dartmouth Steam Railway GWR 2-8-0T 42XX Class 4277 named *Hercules* brings its train into the heritage line station as viewed from the Network Rail version of Paignton station. (July 2016).

Paignton station is 222 miles and 12 chains (357.52 km) from Paddington via Box.

The journey resumes on the main line towards Plymouth.

**Totnes**

| Date Built | Railway/Design | Platforms | Passengers 2014–2015 | Listed |
|---|---|---|---|---|
| 1923 Signal Box | South Devon Railway/GWR | 2 faces | 0.658 million | Yes S'Box |

Figure 130. The fire at Totnes station building in 1962 may account for the gap between the two buildings on platform 2 now. This station has retained passing loops. (July 2016).

Figure 131. A down HST heads straight through for Plymouth. The original footbridge had been demolished by a wayward track-laying crane jib in 1987. The connection to what had been the Ashburton branch and is now the South Devon Railway is to the left of the rear power car of the HST. (July 2016).

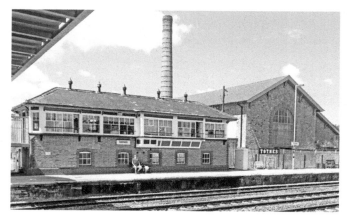

Figure 132. The signal box at Totnes is now a successful café as well as a listed building. The building and chimney to the right are the remains of an atmospheric pumping station that was never used. It is dis-used since Dairy Crest's departure although now listed subsequently. Note the nineteenth-century-style station running in board on the paling fence. (July 2016).

Figure 133. Parcels and luggage moving ancient and modern co-exist together with a Pooley weighbridge for parcels. (July 2016).

Totnes station is 222 miles and 66 chains (358.6 km) from Paddington via Box.

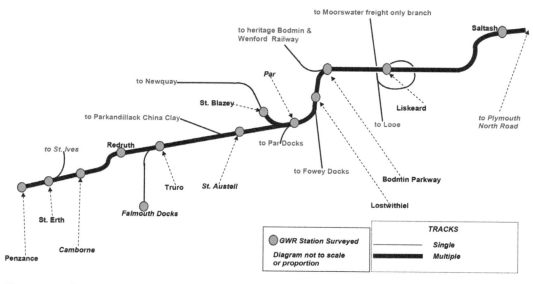

Figure 134. The GWR in Cornwall.

The journey continues after Plymouth North Road station and after the crossing of the River Tamar. Fig. 134 illustrates the Cornish part of the journey from Paddington.

## Saltash

| Date Built | Railway/Design | Platforms | Passengers 2014–2015 | Listed |
|---|---|---|---|---|
| 1880 Rebuilt | Cornwall Railway/GWR | 2 faces | 68,526 | No |

Figure 135. Class 150 150216 gingerly trundles across the Royal Albert Bridge towards Saltash station. (July 2016).

Figure 136. The station building at Saltash has seen better days but is still there without the benefit of listing. The same DMU which just crossed the bridge is headed for Penzance. (July 2016).

Figure 137. Combe-by-Saltash viaduct is just after Saltash station but this HST is Paddington-bound from Penzance. (July 2016).

Saltash station is 251 miles and 26 chains (404.47 km) from Paddington via Box and Plymouth Millbay.

**Liskeard**

| Date Built | Railway/Design | Platforms | Passengers 2014–2015 | Listed |
|---|---|---|---|---|
| 1859/1901 | Cornwall Railway/GWR | 3 faces | 0.357 million | No |

Figure 138. The Brunellian ticket office at Liskeard is at road level and the trains are down below in a cutting. (July 2016).

Figure 139. Class 150 150232 arrives from Plymouth with a service into platform 1 at Liskeard. The connection to the Looe branch is opposite the signal box but Looe trains have their own platform. (July 2016)..

Figure 140. The Class 150 from the previous figure disgorges its passengers and the road is already set for the onward journey to Lostwithiel. The goods shed and yard was on the right. The over bridge is the same one as in the figure of Liskeard ticket office, Fig. 138. (June 2016).

Figure 141. The semaphore signal is known as a gallows bracket and is needed to enable the train driver to see it with the waiting shelter obscuring the view of a conventionally placed signal. (June 2016).

Figure 142. Wessex Trains Class 150 150233 waits for passengers and some of those disembarking will make their way along the path where the camera is to take the Looe train. (April 2004).

Figure 143. At the end of the path is platform 3 for the Looe trains and to the right is the remains of another goods yard and the connection to the main line we saw in Fig. 139. (June 2016).

Figure 144. Platform 3 station building only dates from 1901 so it is a whippersnapper in railway terms. (June 2016).

Liskeard station is 264 miles and 71 chains (426.29 km) from Paddington via Box and Plymouth Millbay.

**Bodmin Parkway**

| Date Built | Railway/Design | Platforms | Passengers 2014–2015 | Listed |
|---|---|---|---|---|
| 1887 Signal Box | Cornwall Railway/GWR | 2 faces | 0.238 million | No |

Figure 145. The venerable footbridge and the signal box, now a café, are the only surviving GWR buildings here. The HST is bound for Penzance on the down main line. (June 2016).

Figure 146. The branch to Bodmin station wends its way across the bridge and some of the Bodmin and Wenford heritage line's rolling stock is in the yard. (October 2004).

Bodmin Parkway station is 274 miles and 3 chains (426.29 km) from Paddington via Box and Plymouth Millbay.

**Lostwithiel**

| Date Built | Railway/Design | Platforms | Passengers 2014–2015 | Listed |
|---|---|---|---|---|
| 1893 Signal Box | Cornwall Railway/GWR | 2 faces | 68,240 | Yes S'Box |

Figure 147. Wessex Trains Class 150 150263 has the road west for Par and beyond. The left-hand arm of the bracket signal controls access to the Fowey Docks line. Imerys Pigments china clay wagons are in the siding. (October 2004).

Figure 148. Looking eastwards at Lostwithiel and the signal box is cited by Historic England as being essentially complete. The ground signal is for a reversing move into the up goods loop. (June 2016).

Figure 149. FGW Class 150 150124 coasts alongside platform 1 for a service stop and the caption above the driver's head announces 'Plymouth'. (June 2016).

Figure 150. East of the station are two goods loops and the up one is in view with the shorter armed signal. The down loop is accessed by courtesy of the shorter armed bracket signal. Down is towards Penzance. (June 2016).

Lostwithiel station is 277 miles and 36 chains (446.51 km) from Paddington via Box and Plymouth Millbay.

**Par**

| Date Built | Railway/Design | Platforms | Passengers 2014–2015 | Listed |
|---|---|---|---|---|
| 1859 Rebuilt 1879 | Cornwall Railway/GWR | 3 faces | 0.278 million | Yes S'Box |

Figure 151. The main station building at Par is not over-large for a junction station but attractive nonetheless. (October 2004).

Figure 152. The scene west towards St Austell sees the line snaking and climbing. The branch line to Newquay is on the right. (September 2014).

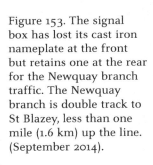

Figure 153. The signal box has lost its cast iron nameplate at the front but retains one at the rear for the Newquay branch traffic. The Newquay branch is double track to St Blazey, less than one mile (1.6 km) up the line. (September 2014).

Figure 154. EWS branded Class 67 67012 heads off for Exeter with a special train off the Newquay branch. The goods yard was behind the coaches. (October 2004).

Figure 155. Plenty of Great Westernry inside the listed Par signal box. There is: cast iron door plate at the end, brown linoleum, lever frame, block and other instruments. Plenty of brass and polish is evident, and an obvious pride in the job. (2014).

Par station is 281 miles and 66 chains (453.55 km) from Paddington via Box and Plymouth Millbay.

**St Blazey**

| Date Built | Railway/Design | Platforms | Passengers 2014–2015 | Listed |
|---|---|---|---|---|
| 1876 | Cornwall Minerals Railway/GWR | 2 faces | Nil – Closed | No |

84

Figure 156. To the right of St Blazey signal box is the down platform for St Blazey station. The station closed in 1925, re-opened until 1934 and was then used by workers' trains. The signal in the foreground controls the up line to Par. (September 2014).

Figure 157. The wagon repair shops at St Blazey keep company with a turntable and roundhouse shed from steam days. China clay, oil tankers for the locos, and ballast wagons are on site. (October 2004).

St Blazey station is 282 miles and 19 chains (454.22 km) from Paddington via Box and Plymouth Millbay.

**St Austell**

| Date Built | Railway/Design | Platforms | Passengers 2014–2015 | Listed |
|------------|----------------|-----------|----------------------|--------|
| 1882 | GWR | 2 faces | 0.468 million | Yes |

Figure 158. The timber station building on platform 2 at St Austell is thought to date from 1882 and is listed, as is the footbridge. This platform services trains to Par and points east. (October 2004).

Figure 159. The signal box only dates from 1906 but is closed and is retained as an office. (October 2004).

St Austell station is 286 miles and 26 chains (460.8 km) from Paddington via Box and Plymouth Millbay.

**Truro**

| Date Built | Railway/Design | Platforms | Passengers 2014–2015 | Listed |
|---|---|---|---|---|
| 1897 Rebuilt | Cornwall Railway/GWR | 3 faces | 1.257 million | No |

Figure 160. French pavilion-style roofs and ironwork at Truro and a BR addition. (October 2004).

Figure 161. Truro looking east. The bay platform 1 for Falmouth is on the extreme right underneath the longer canopy. There was a platform 4 on the extreme left. (September 2014).

Figure 162. Class 150 150216 waits to depart from platform 1 for Falmouth. (September 2014).

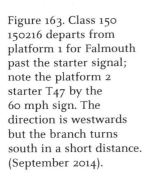

Figure 163. Class 150 150216 departs from platform 1 for Falmouth past the starter signal; note the platform 2 starter T47 by the 60 mph sign. The direction is westwards but the branch turns south in a short distance. (September 2014).

Figure 164. The eastern view sees the signal box with a busy road crossing to deal with as well as train control. (October 2004).

Figure 165. A HST set departs for Penzance past the fibre optic banner repeater signal for the platform starter T47 on the left of the train. (June 2016).

Truro station is 300 miles and 63 chains (483.91 km) from Paddington via Box and Plymouth Millbay.

**Falmouth Docks**

| Date Built | Railway/Design | Platforms | Passengers 2014–2015 | Listed |
|---|---|---|---|---|
| 1897 Rebuilt | GWR | 1 face | 0.137 million | No |

Figure 166. The narrow platform at Falmouth Docks sports a rounded canopy, which was favoured by the GWR where space was tight. The waiting area is visible between the first two pillars. (October 2004).

Falmouth Docks station is 312 miles and 46 chains (503.04 km) from Paddington via Box and Plymouth Millbay.

**Redruth**

| Date Built | Railway/Design | Platforms | Passengers 2014–2015 | Listed |
|---|---|---|---|---|
| 1888 Rebuild | West Cornwall/GWR | 2 faces | 0.344 million | Yes |

Figure 167. The two listed buildings on the site, namely the waiting shelter and footbridge, both date from 1888. (October 2004).

Figure 168. The main station building's service is shorter as it was built in the cash-strapped 1930s. Note 'Platform 3' on the sign: this is in reference to the bus stop outside. (October 2004).

Redruth station is 309 miles and 68 chains (498.65 km) from Paddington via Box and Plymouth Millbay.

## Camborne

| Date Built | Railway/Design | Platforms | Passengers 2014–2015 | Listed |
|---|---|---|---|---|
| 1895 Rebuild | Hayle/GWR | 2 faces | 0.280 million | No |

Camborne station is 313 miles and 40 chains (504.53 km) from Paddington via Box and Plymouth Millbay.

Figure 169. Roskear Junction signal box controls the line that includes Camborne station but now has neither semaphore signals nor indeed a junction. There are no points here either and the crossover near the box is clipped and padlocked out of use. (October 2004).

Figure 170. Camborne station building is an oddity in that it has neither canopy nor evidence of one and seems to be at an angle to the running lines. The goods shed in the distance is now a kitchen warehouse. (October 2004).

| Date Built | Railway/Design | Platforms | Passengers 2014–2015 | Listed |
|---|---|---|---|---|
| 1852 and later | West Cornwall GWR | 4 faces | 0.391 million | Yes |

Figure 171. Historic England describes the station building at St Erth as 'virtually complete and unaltered since built'. (June 2016).

Figure 172. The other side of the station building at St Erth reveals the St Ives branch, platform 3, and what looks like a dock for loading milk churns, long since disused, as platform 4. The main line platforms are to the left. (June 2016).

Figure 173. The main line platforms looking west and the St Ives Bay line on the right. Note the massive canopies for the St Ives side as opposed to the main line to Penzance on the left. (June 2016).

Figure 174. The unique canopy at St Erth is formed because of the steps down to the branch bay platform. The wooden enclosed shelters for passengers and the fact that the canopy is continued the other side of the station building are distinctive features. (September 2014).

Figure 175. The way to Penzance and an HST is expected. See the stop markers for eight, ten, eleven and twelve-coach trains for platform 1. The St Ives portion of the Cornish Riviera Express could be eleven coaches in the 1950s. Note there is bi-directional semaphore signalling. (June 2016).

Figure 176. A view to the east and the down semaphore signal on the right is 'off'. The bracket signal controls the up main line (right) towards Paddington and access to the St Ives branch (left). Platform 3 has its own starter signal on the extreme left. (June 2016).

St Erth station is 320 miles and 78 chains (516.66 km) from Paddington via Box and Plymouth Millbay.

## Penzance

| Date Built | Railway/Design | Platforms | Passengers 2014–2015 | Listed |
|------------|----------------|-----------|----------------------|--------|
| 1879 and later | West Cornwall/ William L. Owen | 4 faces | 0.55 million | No |

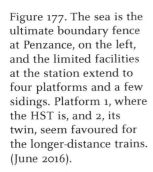

Figure 177. The sea is the ultimate boundary fence at Penzance, on the left, and the limited facilities at the station extend to four platforms and a few sidings. Platform 1, where the HST is, and 2, its twin, seem favoured for the longer-distance trains. (June 2016).

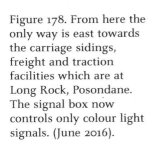

Figure 178. From here the only way is east towards the carriage sidings, freight and traction facilities which are at Long Rock, Posondane. The signal box now controls only colour light signals. (June 2016).

Figure 179. The station building at Penzance, constructed of Cornish granite, does not seem to be going anywhere in the next few hundred years. (June 2016).

Figure 180. The GWR Class 150, 150232, has reached the buffer stops at platform 3 at Penzance station and so in a sense have we in this book.

Penzance station is 326 miles and 50 chains (525.65 km) from Paddington via Box and Plymouth Millbay.